"Amy Carmichael has been one of my heroes of the faith since I first read her biography in college. I'm thrilled to see this excellent new children's book, and I hope Amy's story will inspire and encourage a new generation of children who prayerfully ask God to do great things!"

MELISSA KRUGER, Director of Women's Initiatives, The Gospel Coalition

"This is such an inspiring and engaging book! As kids learn about Amy Carmichael's life, they will see the amazing things God can do when we are faithful to follow him."

ELIZABETH WOODSON, Bible Teacher; Author

"A small book that offers kids a big gospel vision for what God is doing around the world! In its pages, your child will learn that God gives us everything we need to follow his call on our lives."

AMY GANNETT, Founder, Tiny Theologians

"A small book about a big heart. Amy's self-giving love shines in striking contrast to our era of self-love. Turn these pages with your kids and watch them glimpse what life is all about."

MATT SMETHURST, Lead Pastor, River City Baptist Church; Editor, The Gospel Coalition

"Throughout my childhood, God used biographies to instill in me a desire to love and serve Christ with all my heart. Among those was the life of Amy Carmichael. I'm so grateful to Hunter for sharing Amy's story to inspire a new generation with this example of radical faith and sacrificial love."

NANCY DEMOSS WOLGEMUTH, Founder, Revive Our Hearts

"This generation needs countercultural stories about the strength that is found in depending on God through prayer and the assurance in knowing that trusting God's will is always better than anything we could ever dream of! That is what this story is about!"

BETSY GOMEZ, Leader, Revive Our Hearts Hispanic Outreach

"Through Hunter's retelling of Amy Carmichael's story we learn that God speaks to us and that he hears and answers our prayers in his way and in his timing."

KRISTIE ANYABWILE, Author, *Literarily*

Amy Carmichael | © Hunter Beless 2023

Illustrated by Héloïse Mab | Design and Art Direction by André Parker

Series Concept by Laura Caputo-Wickham

Published in association with the literary agency of Wolgemuth & Associates

"The Good Book For Children" is an imprint of The Good Book Company Ltd.

thegoodbook.com | thegoodbook.co.uk | thegoodbook.com.au

thegoodbook.co.nz | thegoodbook.co.in

ISBN: 9781784988203 | Printed in India

thegoodbook
for children

Amy Carmichael

The Brown-Eyed Girl Who Learned to Pray

Hunter Beless

Illustrated by Héloïse Mab

Amy Carmichael had brown eyes, though she wished they were blue.

She begged God to change their color, but peering into the mirror, it didn't seem like he'd heard her prayer. She did so want blue eyes!

Amy started her life in a small village in Ireland. She loved to paint, ride ponies, and cause mischief! But then she was sent away to a school in England.

While she was away, she found herself thinking about her mother's favorite hymn, "Jesus Loves Me." She loved the lines "Jesus loves me, this I know, for the Bible tells me so. Little ones to him belong; we are weak, but he is strong." Amy realized that Jesus had died for her sins and that her life was made for him.

After she moved back to Ireland, one Sunday after church, Amy and her brothers saw a poor, old woman shouldering a heavy bundle, so they stopped to help.

Amy's cheeks burned with embarrassment when she saw the frowns of people passing by, but Amy knew that God wanted her to love people who were seen as unlovable.

Amy started to care for the "shawlies"—women who had very little money and who wore thin shawls as they worked in local mills. Amy started a meeting for the shawlies in her church, but some church people didn't want to share their space with people who were poor.

Amy asked God for help, and this time, God answered her prayer in just the way she'd asked. He provided a new meeting hall, and Amy named it "The Welcome."

Come one, Come all, to the WELCOME HALL

God had answered Amy's prayers, and so Amy kept asking. She had a special "Ask and Receive" book, where she wrote down all the ways she'd seen God answering her prayers.

One day, when she was turning its pages, one word that Jesus had spoken to his disciples sounded in her head: "Go." Amy promised to spend her life going and telling people about Jesus. She decided to become a missionary.

So, Amy went to Japan and told people about Jesus. One woman listened carefully to the good news that Jesus offers us eternal life... until Amy's fancy, fur gloves caught her attention. She was so fascinated with how different Amy looked that she stopped listening to what Amy said!

After that, Amy swapped her English clothes for a silky Japanese robe. She didn't want people to stop listening to the good news about Jesus just because she looked different.

Though Amy saw many Japanese people believe in Christ, she became ill, and so she had to leave. With many twists, turns, ups, and downs, Amy finally ended up in India.

The language there was very hard to learn, but Amy did it. Because she wanted the people to know she was just like them, she traded her English dresses for a traditional Indian one, so that she looked like everyone else.

Peering into the brown eyes of the Indian people, she shared the same, simple message that had brought her to faith years ago: "Jesus loves you, this I know!" Her brown eyes looked just like everyone else's eyes—and the people were listening!

Suddenly, Amy realized why God had given her brown eyes—so that it would be easier for the people in India to listen to her. Years before, God had answered her prayer for blue eyes in the way he knew would be best!

God brought Amy many more people who desperately needed to hear about the love of Jesus, especially children. Many of them had been sold, kidnapped, or abandoned. So, Amy became a mother to many. Every week, the children would say out loud 1 Corinthians 13:13.

"So now faith, hope, and love abide, these three; but the greatest of these is love."

Her family grew and grew into a small village, which had its own school, gardens, houses, offices, and a place to care for sick people.

Just as she'd always done, Amy prayed and trusted God
to provide for their needs. And just as he'd always done,
God answered.

Amy had learned to trust that God would do great things for his glory, and she only needed to ask. So, ask she did. And great things God did.

Amy Carmichael

1867 – 1951

"The greatest of these is love."

1 Corinthians 13:13

Questions to Think About

1. Which part of Amy's story did you like best?

2. Have you ever heard the song *Jesus Loves Me*? How did knowing the love of Jesus encourage Amy to love others, especially those who were often seen as unlovable? What are some ways that you can love others like Jesus loves you?

3. Amy learned to trust that God answers prayers in the way that he knows is best—even her prayer for blue eyes! What would you like to ask God now? Could you start an "Ask and Receive" book?

4. What ideas does Amy's story give you about how you might serve Jesus when you are older?

5. What is one truth about God that you'd like to remember from this story?

Amy Carmichael

1867 In the small town of Millisle in what is today Northern Ireland, Amy Carmichael was born to David and Catherine Carmichael. She was the oldest of seven children.

1883 During her time at boarding school, while thinking about the hymn "Jesus Loves Me," Amy realized that she could not rely on her parents' beliefs but needed to experience "the mercy of the Good Shepherd." It was then that she came to know and love Jesus as her Lord and Savior.

1892 As Amy read through her "Ask and Receive" prayer journal, the words that Jesus spoke to his disciples in Matthew 28:19, "Go ye," sounded in her head. Later that year, Amy committed to spending her life sharing the good news of the gospel.

1893 Amy left for Japan to begin her life as a missionary. With prayer as her driving force, she and her co-laborer, Misaki San, saw many locals repent and believe in Jesus. Sadly, Amy began to suffer from neuralgia, a condition that caused shooting pain and headaches. Her doctor recommended that she take a long rest. While doing so, Amy felt the Lord leading her to continue her missionary work in Sri Lanka, then known as Ceylon.

1895 Amy's plans suddenly changed when she received news that a dear friend had had a stroke. She left Sri Lanka and returned to England to visit him. Amy decided to continue serving God as a missionary in India instead of returning to Sri Lanka. She left for India at age 27 and never returned.

1898 Amy passed her exam in Tamil, the local language in the region of India where she lived. Two years later, Amy moved to Dohnavur, a Christian village, where she would start the Dohnavur Fellowship.

1901 The first girl whom Amy adopted from slavery in a local temple, Preena, arrived at Dohnavur. Amy became like Preena's mother and would go on to become like a mother to many more orphaned Indian children, many of whom she rescued from slavery.

1931 While touring a medical clinic that was being built, Amy fell into a hole and was severely injured. She never recovered full physical mobility, but from her bed she wrote many books that are still widely read today, such as *If*, *A Rose from Brier*, and *Candles in the Dark*.

1951 Amy died and was buried in the garden at Dohnavur. Her grave is marked by a stone bird table inscribed with the word "Ammai," which means "Mother."

returned to England to visit him. Amy decided to continue serving God as a missionary in India instead of returning to Sri Lanka. She left for India at age 27 and never returned.

1898 Amy passed her exam in Tamil, the local language in the region of India where she lived. Two years later, Amy moved to Dohnavur, a Christian village, where she would start the Dohnavur Fellowship.

1901 The first girl whom Amy adopted from slavery in a local temple, Preena, arrived at Dohnavur. Amy became like Preena's mother and would go on to become like a mother to many more orphaned Indian children, many of whom she rescued from slavery.

1931 While touring a medical clinic that was being built, Amy fell into a hole and was severely injured. She never recovered full physical mobility, but from her bed she wrote many books that are still widely read today, such as *If, A Rose from Brier*, and *Candles in the Dark*.

1951 Amy died and was buried in the garden at Dohnavur. Her grave is marked by a stone bird table inscribed with the word "Ammai," which means "Mother."

NORTH
AMERICA

Ireland

EURO

SOUTH
AMERICA

World Map

Where in the world
did Amy's story
take place?

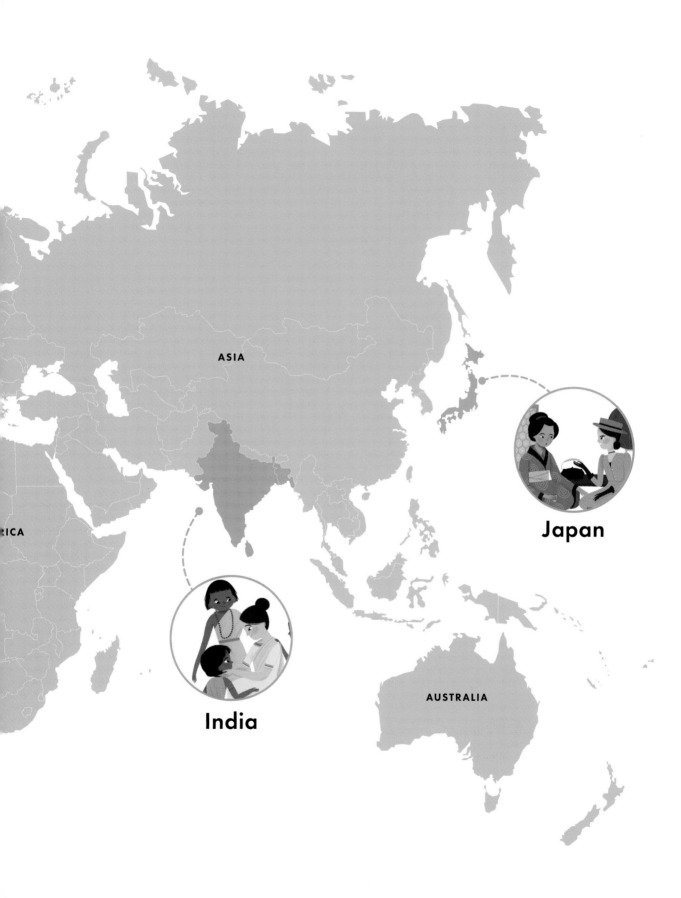

ASIA

Japan

India

AUSTRALIA

Interact With Amy's Story!

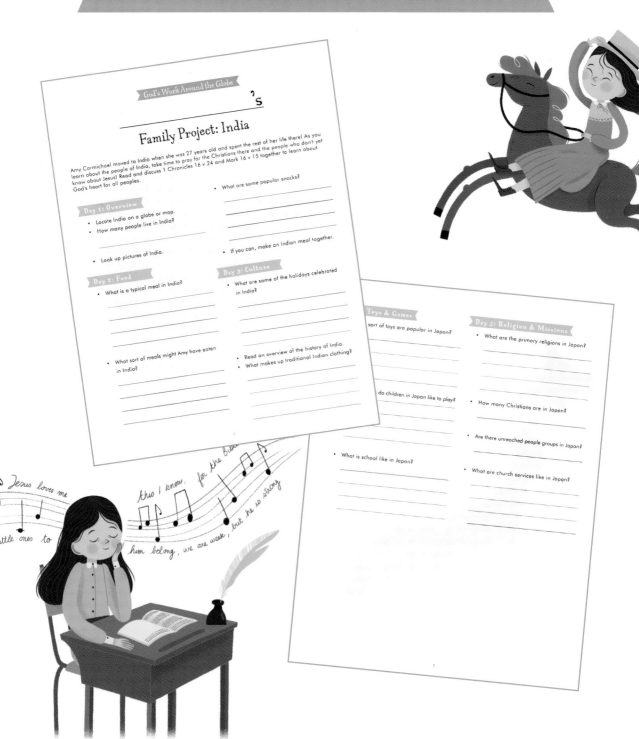

God's Work Around the Globe

_____'s

Family Project: India

Amy Carmichael moved to India when she was 27 years old and spent the rest of her life there! As you learn about the people of India, take time to pray for the Christians there and the people who don't yet know about Jesus! Read and discuss 1 Chronicles 16 v 24 and Mark 16 v 15 together to learn about God's heart for all peoples.

Day 1: Overview
- Locate India on a globe or map.
- How many people live in India?

_____

- Look up pictures of India.

Day 2: Food
- What is a typical meal in India?

_____

- What sort of meals might Amy have eaten in India?

_____

- What are some popular snacks?

_____

- If you can, make an Indian meal together.

Day 3: Culture
- What are some of the holidays celebrated in India?

_____

- Read an overview of the history of India.
- What makes up traditional Indian clothing?

_____

Toys & Games
- What sort of toys are popular in Japan?

_____

- What do children in Japan like to play?

_____

- What is school like in Japan?

_____

Day 5: Religion & Missions
- What are the primary religions in Japan?

_____

- How many Christians are in Japan?

_____

- Are there unreached people groups in Japan?

_____

- What are church services like in Japan?

_____

Jesus loves me this I know, for the Bible tells me so. Little ones to him belong, we are weak, but he is strong.

What Are 8 Things You Liked about Amy's Story?

1.
2.
3.
4.
5.
6.
7.
8.

Remember this Verse Amy Loved

"The greatest of these is love."

1 Corinthians 13 v 13

Can you say it all by yourself?

Family Activity: Sing "Jesus Loves Me" together as a family. Share your favorite worship song and why it is your favorite.

2

8-11s

Biography Report for

Amy Carmichael

By:

My favorite thing about Amy:

Person from the Bible Amy reminds me of:

A question I would ask Amy:

Three words I would use to describe Amy:

1.
2.
3.

Amy Carmichael
Year of

Home

Remember this Verse Amy Loved

"The _____ of _____
is _____."
1 Corinthians 13 v 13

Can you say it 5 times without looking?

Search Online to Find:
Ask an adult about doing this together!

Where in Japan did Amy live?
What did she do there?

How long did Amy spend in Sri Lanka?

What kinds of projects do the Dohnavur Fellowship do now?

1

Download Free Resources at

thegoodbook.com/kids-resources

About the Author

Hunter Beless is passionate about helping women know and love God more, especially through his word. She is the founder of Journeywomen Ministries and the author of *Read it, See it, Say it, Sing it!*, and loves doing ministry in her local church context. You can learn more about Hunter and her family at www.hunterbeless.com.

Do Great Things for God

Inspiring Biographies for Young Children

Corrie ten Boom
The Courageous Woman and the Secret Room
Laura Caputo-Wickham
Illustrated by Isabel Muñoz

Betsey Stockton
The Girl With a Missionary Dream
Laura Caputo-Wickham
Illustrated by Eunji Jung

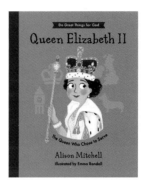

Queen Elizabeth II
The Queen Who Chose to Serve
Alison Mitchell
Illustrated by Emma Randall

Gladys Aylward
The Little Woman With a Big Dream
Laura Caputo-Wickham
Illustrated by Jess Rose

Betty Greene
The Girl Who Longed to Fly
Laura Caputo-Wickham
Illustrated by Héloïse Mab

Fanny Crosby
The Girl Who Couldn't See but Helped the World to Sing
Laura Caputo-Wickham
Illustrated by Jess Rose

Maria Fearing
The Girl Who Dreamed of Distant Lands
K. A. Ellis
Illustrated by Isabel Muñoz

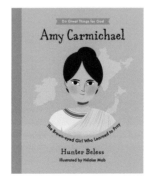

Amy Carmichael
The Brown-eyed Girl Who Learned to Pray
Hunter Beless
Illustrated by Héloïse Mab

Helen Roseveare
The Doctor Who Kept Going No Matter What
Laura Caputo-Wickham
Illustrated by Cecilia Messina

thegoodbook.com | thegoodbook.co.uk